ANTI-INTELLIGENCE

Outsmarting Ourselves in the Age of AI

Erum Katzwan-Rigel

Faith is a quiet abstraction we shaped— not to answer the cosmos, but to hold the fragile, searching human within it. The mystery may live out there. But it is humans who live on Earth— who build the systems, who break them, and who carry the ache of meaning in between.

DEDICATION

To my son, Aarez

who is my strength— a quiet force of light, grounding me in the present and reminding me what matters.

And to the little girl who still lives in me, shy, introverted, endlessly curious. She once sat silently, observing the world, unsure of where she fit— but she never stopped noticing, never stopped thinking. Now, life has brought her to a moment where she can finally bring those quiet thoughts to light— woven with the very technologies reshaping our world.

This book is for both of you:

One who anchors my spirit.

And one who never let it go.

Table of Contents

PREFACE

I didn't write this book to teach you anything.
I wrote it because I could no longer stay silent.

Something is happening—not loud, not sudden, but quiet and corrosive. In our obsession with speed, systems, and synthetic intelligence, we are forgetting how to think for ourselves. We no longer ask "why." We reach for answers before we've understood the question. We swipe before we sit with complexity.

This book is not a guide. It is a resistance.

It exists because I believe the real threat isn't machines replacing us. It's our minds surrendering before they even try.

I grew up in a home with a mosaic floor—scattered fragments of broken stones in all kinds of colors and shapes. As a child, I would lie on that floor and stare, lost in it. At first, it was just randomness. But the longer I looked, the more I began to see: faces, cities, strange patterns. It was a quiet, unexplainable joy—this act of finding sense in chaos.

That simple floor became the beginning of something deeper. Over time, my curiosity for patterns expanded beyond stone and color. I began to see them in human behavior, in systems, in nature, in silence. Later, it became equations in mathematics. Then logic in programming. Then structure in computer science. But at its core, it was always the same thing: a hunger to understand how things connect.

That floor taught me to look. To pause. To notice. It was slow. Quiet. Beautiful. That is what thinking once felt like.

Today, we rarely look. We skim. We scroll. We optimize. But when we move too fast, we lose the patterns that don't shout. We miss the intelligence that whispers.

This book is a pause.

If you are someone who has ever felt that ache—the tension between silence and speed, between knowing and truly understanding—this book is yours.

You won't find comfort here. But you may find something you forgot you had:

The right to question. The courage to think. The permission to wonder.

We need fewer users.

More thinkers.

We need fewer tools.

More principles.

We need fewer shortcuts.

More silence.

This is not a preface. It's a signal.

You are not alone in feeling the tension.

Let's begin.

INTRODUCTION

We are drowning in answers.

Everywhere we turn, something is ready to autocomplete our thoughts—an algorithm, a suggestion, a shortcut. But in a world of predictive everything, we've stopped asking the one question that matters:

Are we still thinking at all?

This is not about Artificial Intelligence. It's about what we're letting go of in its shadow: ambiguity, struggle, attention, depth.

We used to learn by touching the edges of what we didn't know. Now, we learn by clicking the first result.

We used to map the world by trial, error, and lived experience. Now, we inherit maps—optimized, curated, flat.

We used to trust the long way around.

Now we optimize for the smoothest path and call it progress.

But something is wrong. You feel it.

The systems we've built are fast, but hollow. Powerful, but shallow. The further we move into the age of intelligence, the less intelligence we seem to exercise.

This is not a complaint.

It's a challenge.

Anti-Intelligence is not about rejecting technology. It's about reclaiming the parts of us that technology can't replace—if we choose to keep them alive.

This book is short. Because clarity doesn't need length.

It's direct. Because the truth doesn't need decoration.

It's uncomfortable. Because comfort is where intelligence fades.

You've felt it too. Let's go deeper.

CHAPTER 1

The Curve of Human Thought

We are born pattern seekers.

Long before we speak, before we crawl, before we can name the world, we begin to search for order. The human infant stares at a face longer than at a blank wall. A newborn reacts to rhythm. Our earliest instincts are not random; they are architectural. We begin life not in chaos, but in a hunger to decode it.

Pattern is our primal language.

This chapter is a quiet journey—a reflection on how we rise from the floor of randomness to the towers of abstraction, only to risk forgetting how we got there.

Let us begin with a curve. Not a dramatic one, not a line climbing endlessly skyward. Let us begin with a simple function: logarithmic.

$f(x) = \log(x)$

In school, we are taught that a logarithm is the inverse of an exponential. Where exponential growth explodes, logarithmic growth compresses. Each increase in x leads to a smaller and smaller increase in output. It stretches quickly, then levels.

That curve is a metaphor for much more than math. It is the shape of learning.

Phase One: Curiosity

Think of the child who asks "why?" not once, but a hundred times in a day. The adult often becomes exhausted, but the child is just getting started. This is the steep part of the curve—rapid growth, wild input, everything is new.

Why is the sky blue?

Why do I have to sleep?

Why can't I see the air?

This is not idle behavior—it is neural architecture being built in real time. The child is attempting to create internal systems that model the external world.

But eventually, something changes.

We stop asking. Or worse, we are taught to stop.

Phase Two: Efficiency

In adolescence and early adulthood, the curve starts to level. School systems, workplaces, even social environments reward answers, not questions. We are taught to optimize, to solve, to get it right quickly.

Suddenly, questions like "Why is the sky blue?" are replaced by "Will this be on the test?"

We trade the discomfort of confusion for the comfort of clarity. But the price of that clarity is curiosity.

This phase of human thought mirrors the logarithmic curve. The more we learn, the faster we recognize patterns. But the faster we recognize patterns, the less we need to think deeply.

Phase Three: Automation

And then comes automation—not just in machines, but in our minds. We develop mental shortcuts. We know what a conversation sounds like, so we stop listening deeply. We know what a form should look like, so we stop reading carefully.

Software developers recognize this moment well. The first time you write a sorting algorithm, it takes hours of effort. You think through every step. But the tenth time? You import a library.

Efficiency replaces engagement. The mind moves faster, but shallower.

We think we are becoming smarter. But in reality, we are becoming more predictable.

The Hidden Cost of Pattern Mastery

To recognize a pattern is a gift. But to stop questioning it is a curse.

Consider language. A child learning a new word listens to every syllable, repeats it, experiments with its meaning. An adult, fluent in that language, hears words pass like traffic noise.

The poet, however, remains curious. The poet pauses. Rewinds. Explores the space between the syllables.

Pattern mastery without pause becomes blindness.

And in our age—an age of recommendation engines, predictive typing, instant answers—we are drowning in mastery and starving for meaning.

Cognitive Outsourcing

Let's be honest: most of us no longer remember phone numbers. We don't need to. We no longer calculate in our heads. We outsource that to calculators. We no longer read maps. We follow blue dots.

Each tool we adopt is a marvel. It saves time. It improves accuracy. But each tool also takes something from us: the need to remember, the need to reason, the need to explore.

This is not about nostalgia. It is about neurological muscle.

The less we use it, the weaker it gets.

Are We Getting Smarter?

That is the paradox.

We are producing more knowledge than ever. But fewer people understand it deeply. We are making systems more powerful than anything our ancestors could imagine. But fewer people can explain how they work.

We are climbing the exponential curve of capability. But we are flattening the logarithmic curve of cognition.

A Personal Reflection

I remember, as a girl, staring at the floor made of broken stone. The pattern was random—stone chips of different shapes, colors, and textures. But I would stare long enough until faces appeared. Mountains. Maps. Stories.

That was my first training in pattern recognition. And it came not from a machine. It came from silence. From boredom. From the luxury of unstructured thought.

Today, I rarely stare at floors. I stare at screens.

I type. I scroll. I search. But do I still see?

Anti-Intelligence: A Quiet Warning

This chapter is not an accusation. It is a whisper. A nudge.

It is asking you, the reader, to consider not just what you know, but how you came to know it.

When was the last time you learned something the hard way? Not Googled it. Not watched a 2-minute video. But struggled. Sat with confusion. Wrestled with the unformed shape of truth.

That is intelligence. And we are losing it.

Anti-intelligence is not stupidity. It is the smooth surface of knowledge that never cracks. It is the algorithm that serves you what you want before you know you want it. It is the silence of the question never asked.

This chapter is the beginning of a deeper curve. One that demands friction. Reflection. Resistance.

A curve that doesn't flatten, but folds back inward—into depth.

Because the future will not be defined by those who consume the most patterns. It will be shaped by those who ask where the patterns came from.

And what might lie beyond them.

CHAPTER 3

The Illusion of Intelligence

We live in an era where intelligence is increasingly defined by performance. How fast a system responds, how well it predicts, how accurately it aligns with expectation. These measurements, though useful, are deceptive. They focus on results, not reasoning. On answers, not understanding. They elevate the illusion of intelligence while slowly eroding its essence.

Let us begin with the most pressing question of our time:

Are intelligent systems truly intelligent—or are they reflections of our collective shortcuts?

Artificial Intelligence is everywhere. It recommends our music, filters our spam, powers our navigation, grades our tests, and even writes our essays. It is branded as smart. But behind every smart system is a framework of decisions—most of them made by humans, some by models trained on human data, and all rooted in probabilities.

The intelligence we observe is not alive. It does not think. It processes. It predicts.

We are projecting the word "intelligence" onto behaviors that match our expectations. That's not necessarily wrong—but it is incomplete.

Intelligence, in its truest form, involves awareness. Self-reflection. The ability to choose what not to do. Machines don't do that. They optimize for goals we define. They don't ask whether the goal is worth pursuing.

This distinction is not philosophical fluff. It matters deeply in how we design, use, and evaluate these systems.

Let's pause on a core concept: proxies.

A proxy is a stand-in, a substitute. In machine learning, proxies are everywhere. Want to measure happiness? Use emoji usage. Want to measure productivity? Count keystrokes. Want to assess understanding? Track how long a student stays on a page.

These proxies are seductive. They give us numbers. Dashboards. Visualizations. But they don't give us truth.

We are mistaking the map for the terrain.

This happens in human systems too. Universities use GPA as a proxy for intelligence. Companies use job titles as a proxy for competence. Social platforms use followers as a proxy for influence. These proxies simplify evaluation. But they flatten nuance.

The more we rely on proxies, the more we drift from meaning. And as AI systems scale, they inherit our proxies. They absorb our approximations. They accelerate our assumptions.

This is not intelligence. This is compression.

Compression is not inherently bad. It is, in fact, one of the most powerful tools in nature. DNA is compressed code. Language is compressed experience. Culture is compressed history. But compression always loses something. Always.

So when we build AI systems that compress decision-making, we must ask: what are we losing?

Let's consider a thought experiment:

Imagine a student uses an AI system to write an essay. The output is grammatically flawless, logically coherent, and well-structured. The teacher grades it an A. But the student learned nothing. They didn't wrestle with the material. They didn't structure their own argument. They didn't experience the discomfort of unclear thought becoming clear.

Now multiply this across a generation.

What kind of thinkers are we producing?

What kind of citizens?

The illusion of intelligence becomes dangerous when it is rewarded equally to real intelligence. When outputs become indistinguishable from understanding.

This is happening across disciplines.

In design: templates replace composition.

In coding: frameworks replace logic.

In education: testing replaces exploration.

In leadership: charisma replaces clarity.

We are elevating surfaces over substance.

But let's be careful. This is not a call to reject modern tools. It's a call to use them mindfully. Intelligently.

An artist using AI to extend their creativity is still an artist.

A developer leveraging a framework to accelerate delivery is still a developer.

The difference is awareness. Intentionality.

Are you outsourcing to accelerate—or to avoid?

Are you using the tool—or being shaped by it?

Because here's the hidden cost of the illusion: when tools become too easy, they make hard thinking feel unnecessary. And hard thinking is the gym of intelligence.

Let's dive into an example from education.

There's a growing movement of students using chatbots to answer homework questions. The tools are effective. They provide instant answers. But over time, students report decreased confidence in problem-solving. They no longer trust their own minds. They become dependent on the shortcut.

We must ask: what happens when the shortcut becomes the default route?

That question echoes in every domain.

In journalism, AI writes headlines. But who decides what's important?

In science, models simulate results. But who questions the assumptions?

In justice, algorithms suggest sentences. But who sees the full human story?

The illusion of intelligence is seductive because it delivers results without the burden of thought. But without thought, there is no transformation.

Real intelligence transforms us.

It leaves us different than it found us.

It humbles. It sharpens. It connects.

So what do we do?

First, we must name the illusion.

We must stop equating functionality with understanding.

We must separate fluency from depth.

We must resist the temptation to automate the very things that make us human: questioning, reflecting, struggling, growing.

Second, we must teach the difference.

In schools, we must reward the process, not just the result.

In workplaces, we must value clarity, not just speed.

In culture, we must elevate the thinkers, not just the influencers.

And third, we must model it.

We—parents, teachers, builders, leaders—must show what real intelligence looks like.

Not perfection.

Not polish.

But presence.

The willingness to say, "I don't know."

The courage to ask, "What are we missing?"

The discipline to go slower when it matters.

Because in the race to appear intelligent, we risk becoming artificial ourselves.

This chapter is an invitation:

To think when it's easier not to.

To pause when momentum is pushing you forward.

To remember that the mind is not just a processor—it's a question mark wrapped in neurons.

And questions, not answers, are the birthplace of every leap forward.

CHAPTER 4

When Everything Becomes A Platform

There was a time when software was built for a single purpose. A tool did one thing. A calculator calculated. A notepad took notes. A camera captured images. The boundaries were clear. The intention was specific. But today, software does not exist in isolation. It exists inside ecosystems. Inside frameworks. Inside platforms.

Everything is a platform now.

The word 'platform' has become both omnipresent and ambiguous. It is used to describe cloud infrastructure, social networks, design systems, operating environments, and business models. Platforms have evolved from being static containers of tools to becoming dynamic environments where tools are built, connected, shared, monetized, and scaled.

But what happens when every tool is a platform? What happens when we no longer build from scratch, but only assemble from existing parts?

This chapter explores the architecture of platforms—not in code, but in thought. Because platforms don't just shape how we build—they shape how we think.

Let us begin with a definition.

A platform, in its most basic sense, is a foundation upon which other things are built. It provides structure, rules, and interfaces. In the digital world, platforms abstract complexity and offer modularity. They allow developers to plug into ecosystems. They allow users to experience seamlessness.

But beneath that elegance is a trade-off: the more we rely on platforms, the more we conform to their assumptions.

Take a developer building a mobile app. In the past, this would require low-level understanding: memory management, device-specific quirks, rendering logic. Today, using a platform like Flutter or React Native, the developer can build cross-platform apps without thinking deeply about these concerns.

This is empowering.

But it is also limiting.

The developer now operates within the boundaries of the platform's design. They inherit its limitations, its architectural biases, its lifecycle choices. They build faster—but understand less.

The same applies to design. A UI designer today can leverage design systems like Material or Carbon. They don't need to rethink button styles or input spacing. This increases consistency. It reduces decision fatigue. But it also reduces exploration.

What happens to creativity when every design begins with a template?

Platforms reward conformity. That's how they scale. But true intelligence often requires divergence.

There is also a socio-economic dimension to this shift.

Platforms centralize power. A few companies own the infrastructure. Others build on top of it. The more powerful the platform, the more difficult it becomes to build outside it. Developers, businesses, and even governments become dependent.

This is not dystopia. It is a design choice. But one that must be examined.

Because when everything becomes a platform, innovation becomes layered abstraction. We stop building base systems. We stop questioning fundamentals. We start to assume the platform is the ground.

But it is not the ground. It is a surface laid upon older surfaces, often brittle and undocumented. The platform abstracts the past, but the past does not disappear. It lingers. It shapes.

There is a generational effect too.

New engineers often begin their journey inside platforms. They learn through interfaces, SDKs, sandboxed environments. They become masters of tools they did not build. They gain speed, but not roots.

Imagine teaching architecture only through prefab kits. Students might become excellent assemblers—but lose the intuition of weight, tension, material, space.

This is happening in code.

In thought.

In systems.

When platforms become the default environment for learning and building, we risk raising generations of professionals who are fluent but fragile.

Fluent in patterns. Fragile in principles.

So what is the alternative?

It is not to reject platforms. That is neither feasible nor desirable. Platforms enable extraordinary things. They democratize access. They reduce barriers. They accelerate.

But they must be balanced with something deeper: platform literacy.

Platform literacy means understanding what lies beneath. It means tracing the layers. It means asking:

Who built this?

What assumptions does it carry?

What happens if I step outside of it?

It also means building from scratch—at least once. Writing your own server. Designing your own protocol. Sketching your own system architecture without relying on pre-built patterns. Not because it's efficient. But because it's educational.

Education without experience is fragile. And experience without friction is shallow.

Platforms remove friction. That's their promise. But intelligence grows in friction.

When everything becomes a platform, we must choose to go beneath.

To break things open.

To trace dependencies.

To name the assumptions.

Because platforms shape more than code. They shape cognition.

And when cognition conforms, anti-intelligence begins.

This chapter is a map. A reminder.

That the path to understanding is not just through assembly—but through disassembly.

Through asking not just how it works, but why it was built that way.

Through remembering that a platform is not the destination.

It is the stage.

And intelligence is not just knowing how to perform on it.

It is knowing when—and how—to build your own.

CHAPTER 5

The Curriculum of The Future

Every generation has asked the question: What should we teach the next generation?

But never before has that question been so uncertain, so unsettled, so full of ambiguity. In a world changing at the pace of algorithms, globalized systems, artificial intelligence, and rapid abstraction, education is no longer just about content—it is about capability.

And yet, we continue to design our education systems with the assumption that the world will stay still long enough for students to catch up.

This chapter explores what a truly intelligent curriculum of the future might look like—not just for schools, but for society. Because in the age of anti-intelligence, the way we teach will determine not just what we know, but who we become.

Let us begin with a scene.

A classroom. A teacher at the front. Students in rows. A whiteboard. A projector. Perhaps some laptops. The curriculum? Mathematics, science, language, history. The structure? One year, one subject, one test. The goal? Understanding and passing.

This structure has remained largely unchanged for over a century.

But the world outside the classroom has changed beyond recognition.

AI now generates content faster than teachers can grade it.

Students use language models to complete essays they haven't read.

Computers debug code better than junior developers.

In this world, what is the purpose of memorization?

Of repetition?

Of surface learning?

What should education teach when information is infinite and instantly accessible?

Let us offer a different vision.

Imagine a curriculum based not on answers, but on questions.

A system where students are not measured by how much they retain, but how deeply they inquire. Where tests are not closed-book, but open-ended. Where the teacher is not a source of truth, but a facilitator of exploration.

Imagine a curriculum built around paradoxes:

- Why does abstraction help—and hurt?
- How does intelligence grow—and shrink?
- What makes something worth learning?

This is not fantasy. It is a call.

Because anti-intelligence begins the moment curiosity is replaced by compliance.

What Should We Teach?

Here are five domains that must shape the curriculum of the future:

1. Pattern Thinking

Not just pattern recognition, but the ability to connect seemingly unrelated domains. To find structure in chaos. To understand that patterns are not only in math, but in music, culture, society, and systems.

2. Abstraction Literacy

To trace layers. To understand what's hidden. To reverse-engineer. To know when to rely on abstraction—and when to dig deeper. To ask, "What am I not seeing?"

3. Systemic Ethics

Not moralism, but systems thinking applied to consequences. How does a decision ripple through a system? What are the unintended consequences? How do we build tools that don't just work—but work responsibly?

4. Cognitive Resilience

The ability to tolerate confusion. To sit with uncertainty. To unlearn. To rebuild. To understand that thinking is not a performance, but a process.

5. Creative Engineering

To make things from scratch. To solve real problems. To design systems with intentional friction. To reimagine tools, not just use them.

Each of these domains could be a lifelong journey.

And yet, they are almost completely absent from our current systems.

Why?

Because they don't fit into neat assessments.

Because they don't scale easily.

Because they are slow.

But so is intelligence.

The Danger of Curriculum Without Depth

When we teach only what is measurable, we produce minds that are efficient—but brittle.

When we teach only what is current, we forget what is timeless.

When we teach only what can be tested, we abandon what must be questioned.

The irony is this: in our obsession with preparing students for the future, we are failing to prepare them for the present.

Because the present is already abstract, modular, fast, and automated.

Students are growing up inside platforms, surrounded by predictive algorithms, immersed in digital ecosystems. But few are being taught how those systems work. Fewer still are being taught to question them.

This is not a failure of teachers.

It is a failure of design.

We are building curricula that reflect the world as it was—not as it is.

And in doing so, we are cultivating anti-intelligence: a silent erosion of depth, curiosity, and courage.

What Will Replace the Hello World?

In programming, students have long been taught to begin with "Hello, world!"—a simple exercise to print a line of text to the screen. It is iconic. Simple. Universal.

But is it enough?

Today's new programmers start not with syntax—but with libraries, frameworks, scaffolding tools, and pre-trained models. They start higher up the abstraction chain.

What happens when the first step is no longer foundational?

We must ask: What is the new Hello World?

Perhaps it is building your own server.

Writing your own compiler.

Designing your own encryption algorithm.

Not because these are practical—but because they teach roots.

Roots are what prevent collapse.

In a storm, shallow systems fall.

A New Kind of School

Imagine a school that teaches from the inside out.

Where every subject connects to every other.

Where math is not taught in isolation, but as a tool for philosophy, economics, and art.

Where history is not a list of dates, but a study of decisions, patterns, and consequences.

Where students are taught to question the interface.

To peel back the layer.

To trace the architecture of the world around them.

Where intelligence is not defined by speed—but by clarity.

Not by output—but by insight.

Not by polish—but by perspective.

This school does not yet exist.

But pieces of it do.

In labs. In after-school programs. In homes. In communities. In conversations like this one.

And if we do not build it, we must ask: what will be left?

A generation raised to use tools they cannot repair.

To answer questions they do not understand.

To perform intelligence without practicing it.

That is the final exam of our time.

And we must not fail it.

CHAPTER 6

Intelligence In Decline—Automation And The Human Mind

It begins quietly.

A tool suggests the next word. A browser fills in the form. A car keeps its lane. A device completes your sentence. The feeling is subtle, almost magical. You're not doing less. You're just doing it faster. But then, something shifts.

You forget how to write a strong sentence without suggestions.

You don't bother learning your friend's number.

You stop reading full articles.

This is the slow erosion of active thought. Not because we lack intelligence—but because intelligence is being replaced by automation.

This chapter examines the paradox: as we build more powerful systems, we require less powerful minds to operate them. And in doing so, we risk cultivating not stupidity, but something more dangerous: dependency without awareness.

Let us begin with a principle: automation is not inherently anti-intelligent. In fact, it is born from intelligence. The desire to simplify, optimize, and delegate is what drives innovation. But the problem is not in the automation—it is in how we relate to it.

There are three stages of automation:

1. Assistance – The system helps you do your task better.
2. Delegation – The system does the task for you.
3. Dependence – You can no longer do the task without the system.

Every innovation begins in stage one, but many end in stage three.

Think of GPS. It began as a helpful tool—assistance. Then it took over our route planning—delegation. Today, many of us would be lost—literally—without it. We have offloaded spatial reasoning, orientation, and memory.

What else are we offloading?

We offload calculation to calculators.

Memory to phones.

Decision-making to algorithms.

Social curation to feeds.

Discovery to recommendations.

In the process, we are building a world where friction is removed—but so is muscle.

Mental muscle.

Cognitive resistance.

The raw effort that forms the foundation of understanding.

This is not nostalgia for a pre-digital age. It is a call to examine the long-term neurological impact of technological convenience.

We know, for example, that hippocampus activity decreases when people rely on GPS. We know that multitasking impairs focus. We know that reading on screens alters comprehension.

But what is less understood is the silent shift in agency.

When a student no longer practices solving equations—because the app solves them for her—what is she learning?

When a developer no longer writes a sorting algorithm—because the framework imports it—what is he mastering?

We are building tools that accelerate our work, but they also atrophy our instincts.

And the more seamless they become, the less we even notice.

This leads to a new kind of intelligence decline—not measured in IQ, but in capability.

The capability to:

- ◆ troubleshoot when systems fail
- ◆ reason without external prompts
- ◆ create from first principles
- ◆ think without instruction

This is not an academic concern. It is a civic one.

In a society where automation drives everything from news to elections, the question is not just who builds the systems—but who understands them. And who questions them.

Because every automated system reflects the bias of its creators.

And if users become too passive, they accept outputs as truth.

That's the birth of compliance. Not through coercion. But through comfort.

Anti-intelligence is not a moment—it is a gradient.

It begins with a helpful nudge.

It ends with silence.

Let us revisit the idea of intelligence.

What is it?

Is it solving problems?

Is it creating ideas?

Is it recognizing patterns?

Is it learning from failure?

All of the above. But more importantly, intelligence is the practice of agency.

It is the decision to act, reflect, adjust, and repeat.

Automation removes steps.

But when it removes decisions, it removes growth.

We must ask: how much can we outsource before we become spectators of our own cognition?

There is a term in software called eventual consistency. It describes a system that doesn't maintain real-time synchronization, but over time, becomes consistent. Our minds are becoming eventually passive. Over time, we stop initiating thought. We respond. We swipe. We accept.

This is the great threat.

Not that automation will become intelligent.

But that we will stop being curious.

Let's look at the workplace.

In many industries, automation is pitched as a way to reduce boring tasks—data entry, scheduling, reporting. And in many ways, it succeeds.

But then, the skills that once required thought are removed from training. New employees don't learn how to calculate by hand. They learn how to operate the tool.

And when the tool changes, they don't adapt—they wait for a new instruction manual.

Resilience is lost.

We are raising a workforce of operators, not designers.

Of consumers, not creators.

Of responders, not initiators.

The promise of AI was augmentation—not replacement.

But when we reduce friction without retraining cognition, we replace silently.

Reclaiming Agency

So what can we do?

1. Redesign learning environments

Create tasks that require friction. Encourage projects without templates. Reward questions, not just answers. Teach students to think around the tool, not just through it.

2. Practice manual thinking

Once a week, solve a problem without digital help. Draw your system architecture by hand. Sketch out the logic of a process before coding it. This is not inefficiency—it is strength training.

3. Cultivate skepticism

When a system gives you an answer, ask: "What is this based on?"

Trace the logic. Challenge the assumption. Break the chain. Not to be contrarian—but to stay awake.

4. Create tool awareness

Every tool has a history. Every interface is a story. Learn it. Share it. Teach others to see the invisible infrastructure behind what feels automatic.

5. Value slow knowledge

Read long books. Study old systems. Walk instead of scroll. Explore instead of click. Slowness is not the enemy—it is the soil of wisdom.

The future will be automated.

But intelligence must be chosen.

And the mind, like any system, needs maintenance.

Needs challenge.

Needs friction.

This chapter ends with a paradox:

Automation, done right, can free us to think more deeply.

But done blindly, it removes the very need to think.

The line between the two is invisible.

It is drawn by awareness.

And awareness is the last place where intelligence lives.

Don't outsource that.

CHAPTER 7

Beyond Intelligence – Reclaiming Depth In A Patterned World

If you look long enough at the stars, you start to see the past. Not metaphorically, but literally. The light reaching your eyes has traveled years—sometimes centuries, millennia. You are not seeing the stars as they are. You are seeing them as they were.

That delay, that distance, that slowness—that is what makes astronomy a practice of humility. It teaches us that to truly understand, we must look beyond immediacy. We must look beyond what is visible.

This chapter is not about systems, platforms, or automation. It is about something deeper: how to live, think, and feel in a world where intelligence has become performative, patterned, and predictable.

It is about what lies beyond intelligence.

Because intelligence—at least as we define it today—is not enough.

It has become too narrow. Too quantifiable. Too fast. It has been flattened into scores, metrics, and performances. But real intelligence is not efficient. It is not always measurable. It is not always useful.

Sometimes it is slow.

Sometimes it is messy.

Sometimes it is silent.

And often, it is invisible.

What if the next stage of human evolution is not in becoming more intelligent—but more aware? More present? More willing to feel, doubt, and pause?

Let us begin by distinguishing three kinds of intelligence:

1. Performative Intelligence — What we display to others. It is polished, prepared, optimized for visibility. It performs well on tests, interviews, metrics.

2. Practical Intelligence — What we use to navigate the world. It includes habits, heuristics, systems, and learned behaviors. It solves problems efficiently.

3. Philosophical Intelligence — What we use to ask better questions. It is not focused on utility, but on depth. It lives in doubt, wonder, paradox, and silence.

Modern society rewards the first. Sometimes the second. Almost never the third.

But it is the third that makes civilizations endure.

When we talk about anti-intelligence, we are not simply referring to a lack of learning. We are referring to the erosion of the philosophical core of human thought.

It is the erosion of the inner life.

In a world obsessed with results, we have made inner thought obsolete.

We ask children, "What do you want to be?" but rarely, "What do you think about when you're alone?"

We ask job candidates about their experience, but not about their values.

We train minds to perform, but not to dwell.

This is the real crisis.

We have built a civilization of doers—but not reflectors.

Of makers—but not questioners.

Of builders—but not breakers of patterns.

The future does not need more intelligence.

It needs more integration.

Integration of thought and emotion.

Of speed and stillness.

Of systems and soul.

We must learn to ask better questions—not just of machines, but of ourselves.

Where do my beliefs come from?

What am I avoiding when I optimize?

What am I feeling beneath the performance?

These are not abstract questions.

They are architectural.

They shape the very foundation upon which all other intelligence is built.

Let us talk about silence.

Silence is not the absence of noise—it is the presence of space.

It is the condition in which deep thought emerges.

It is the room in which the self becomes visible.

But today, silence is rare.

We fill every gap with content.

Every pause with noise.

Every boredom with a screen.

We are never alone.

And so we never meet ourselves.

To reclaim intelligence, we must reclaim silence.

The philosopher Blaise Pascal once wrote, "All of humanity's problems stem from man's inability to sit quietly in a room alone."

He was right.

A mind that cannot sit still is a mind that cannot think deeply.

Let us also speak of wonder.

Wonder is not curiosity.

It is deeper.

It is the reverent awe of not knowing.

It is the surrender to mystery.

It is the capacity to hold a question without rushing to answer it.

Children know wonder.

Artists pursue it.

Mystics live in it.

But modern education, with its rubrics and schedules, squeezes wonder out.

Modern work, with its deadlines and metrics, suffocates it.

We must return to wonder.

Not because it is productive—but because it is human.

The most intelligent people I have ever met are not the fastest, nor the loudest, nor the most decorated.

They are the ones who ask the most beautiful questions.

They are the ones who can sit with uncertainty.

They are the ones who make space for others to think.

They are philosophers of their own lives.

We all must become that.

Because the systems we are building are accelerating.

But humans do not accelerate well.

We are built for rhythm, not speed.

For cycles, not sprints.

The more we automate, the more we must humanize.

The more we abstract, the more we must ground.

The more we perform, the more we must pause.

Beyond intelligence lies a deeper virtue: attention.

To pay attention—not just with the eyes, but with the whole self.

To see not just what is, but what is becoming.

To listen—not for reply, but for resonance.

That is the antidote to anti-intelligence.

A return to presence.

A return to roots.

A return to the quiet revolution of asking:

What kind of human do I want to be?

Because intelligence alone cannot answer that.

Only attention can.

Only wonder can.

Only you can.

This chapter is the final whisper before the conclusion.

Not a summary.

Not a command.

But a hand extended, inviting you to walk back into your own mind.

Not to optimize it.

Not to measure it.

Not to automate it.

But simply to dwell in it.

Because beyond intelligence is not ignorance.

It is soul.

CONCLUSION

You won't find a checklist here. No 10-step recovery plan for your brain. No hack to bring your curiosity back.

Because what you need isn't more input.

It's subtraction. Silence. Resistance.

The threat of anti-intelligence isn't obvious. It doesn't arrive like a virus or a crash. It arrives as comfort. Convenience. An app that knows what you want. A tool that thinks before you do. A moment of uncertainty, erased too quickly.

We are told to trust the interface.

Trust the algorithm.

Trust the system.

But trust without questioning is not trust. It's dependency.

And dependency is the death of thought.

You are not a user. You are a thinker.

Not a node. A mind.

Ask the question even if you already know the answer.

Take the long way once in a while.

Break a perfect process to remember that you are not a machine.

We don't need more artificial intelligence.

We need less artificiality in our intelligence.

Reclaim the pause. Reclaim the edge.

Not to go backward.

But to go inward.

That's where thinking begins again.

ACKNOWLEDGEMENTS

This book was written in solitude, but it is made of everyone who crossed my path—through inspiration, challenge, silence, or kindness.

To my son, who is my strength and compass. Your light keeps me grounded in this ever-accelerating world.

To those who asked questions I wasn't ready to answer—and those who waited while I found the words.

To the quiet thinkers, the misfits, the slow-readers, and the pattern-watchers—this book speaks in your language.

And to everyone who still believes that thought is sacred, silence is powerful, and wonder is worth protecting—

Thank you for reminding me I am not alone.